Something Smells Like Pee

and Other Classy Observations

By

Blythe E. Jewell

ISBN: 1481215620
ISBN-13: 978-1481215626

DEDICATION

For my son Sam. Even though you're not allowed to read any of this until you're at least 18. Possibly older. Maybe never.

I love you more than the sun and the moon and the stars and the sky and the earth and everything on it. And I always, always will.

Mom

CONTENTS

ACKNOWLEDGMENTS

Thanks to my mom, Kathie Jewell, for her love, support and unwavering faith in me, despite all my ridiculous fuck-ups.

Thanks to my dad, Jim Jewell, for being a great Papa, and my stepmom, Maureen Boggs Jewell, for her enormous laugh (which still scares the bejezus out of me sometimes). Also to my sister Sarah and my grandma Estelle, who's 96 and still kickin' it homestyle.

Thanks to my BFF Leigh Cook, who keeps me going every day and always manages to find the silver lining – even when I totally don't want to hear that shit. And also to Jen Burford, who's the strongest person I know. Without you two, I'm pretty sure I'd die.

Thanks to friends Wendi Aarons (wendiaarons.com) and Peyton Price (suburbanhaiku.com) for reading this book in its hideous draft form and offering gentle critiques like, "Yeah, that's stupid," and, "Seriously, don't fucking do that." Also to Jennifer Sutton (@thesearenewdays), whose weeklong delay in reading it made me sick with so much self-doubt I wanted to kick my own ass.

Thanks to my super talented, wonderful, funny friends Amy McSpadden, Heather Kafka, Becky Klier, Paula Ortiz, Paige Watts, Janine DiSalvo, Ross Hooks, Rhonda Capps, Brooks Wood and many more. You guys inspire me all the time, just by being you.

And a special thanks to my husband Jason Gander, who somehow manages to make me laugh every day (occasionally with stuff shooting out of my nose), even when - sometimes *especially* when - he's being a total douche. I love you, ya big lug.

i

INTRODUCTION

Hi. I'm Blythe. This is my book.

It's not really a *book* so much as a collection of weird stuff I create all the time to keep myself entertained. Thoughts, poems, drawings... random observations of my very normal life as a clueless mom, snarky wife, frustrated driver, sometime office drone and generally reluctant consumer of pop culture.

I'm not really sure why I'm publishing it. Maybe just to say I did. And for the Amazon author's page, obviously – because who *doesn't* want one of those?

Okay, so the only things on it will be this nonsense and an anthology that includes some crappy thing I wrote years ago offering my (totally un)esteemed opinion about slutty lingerie on Valentine's Day. (Spoiler quote: "If naked isn't good enough, we have a problem.") But, whatever. Who cares? I'm a *published author* now, y'all. Just like Emily Dickinson. Or Jane Austen. Or Madonna.

Huh. This could possibly be the shittiest intro ever written. I don't know. There might be worse intros out there, but I don't think I've ever read one. I feel like I should get some kind of Shitty Intro award. Has anyone created one of those yet? Next project!

Well. Anyway. What I'm really trying to say is, thanks for buying my book. I hope you don't think it sucks.

Love,

Blythe

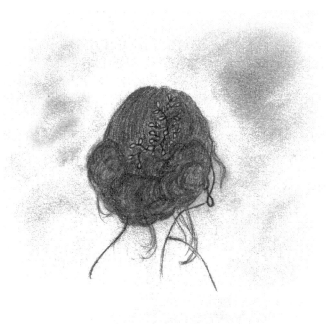

HAIR IN MY ASS CRACK

I wash my hair
I wash my face
I wash my body all over the place
and when I reach that one spot, there...
there's always a glob of hair.

4

As the shampoo rinses
from each long tress
some falls from my head in a graceful mess
I don't notice it trail right down my back
and settle in my ass crack.

Once it reaches
its destination
it jumbles into a knotty formation
and bids goodbye to my crowning dome
as it settles in its new home.

My hands move down
in a cleansing technique;
soapy, they slip between my cheeks
I pull something strange from the dark abyss
and ask, "What the fuck is this?"

I run my hand under
the hot, moist rain
and watch as the glob slides down the drain
I stand there alone in the steamy fog…

and just hope it doesn't clog.

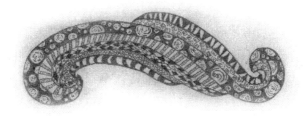

UNFRIENDED

(gasp) (sharp breath)
Out loud, I swear
as I log into Facebook and see you're not there

"I'm fine," I assert
"My feelings aren't hurt."
I tell myself I just don't care.

In the grand scheme of things
I know in my heart
this is not even close to the worst...

But still.
I really,
really,
just *really*
wanted to unfriend you first.

MATT DAMON

I once read a book about
Telepathic Mental Currents
and every day since
I have sent out
Love Vibes that are
very
very
very
strong

Each day I reach out
to him with my love
and all my mental passion

I carefully repeat
my phone number
over and over and over

I don't know why
he hasn't called.

NOT SLEEPING

There's a cramp in my left leg
and a sharp pain in my neck
When I get up in the morning
I'll still feel both, I suspect

There's a leg wrapped 'round my belly
slightly shorter than my own
An elbow jabs and pokes and stabs
between my shoulder bones

A smallish hand is draped across
three quarters of my face
The rest of me clings tightly
to my four inches of space

I can't reach my blinking clock
the light disturbs my eyes
A dog's wet nose nudges my toes
and there's a cat between my thighs

A large man's body spreads out wide
He takes up half the bed
The rest of us are left to squeeze
in tight from toe to head

The snoring's done in tandem
It rattles through my brain
I swear that the cacophony
could drown out a steam train

I lie here in the dark and know
no sleep will come tonight
We're stuffed and jammed
and crushed and crammed --
but still, somehow, it's right.

My baby snuggles in and his
embrace makes my heart swell
So I stay –
loved, happy and
uncomfortable as hell.

THE PEDICURE

You should have known to look out for
my extra tickly place
but still, I'm very sorry that
I kicked you in the face.

SPOILED BY KINDLE

I touch,
with a warm, soft finger
word after
word after
word

But no matter
how determined I am
No matter
how warm my touch
No matter
how hard I press

This paperback book has
no
electronic
dictionary
feature

ON OUR PERIODS TOGETHER

Since we first met, we've been best of friends
Holding each other's hair, time and again
We've stood by each other through thick and through thin
and we're on our periods together.

Our husbands and children are all family, too
They love, laugh and bicker just like we used to
But when Auntie Flo comes they don't know what to do,
'cause we're on our periods together.

Anniversaries, birthdays and family vacations;
together our lives are one big celebration
But our kids fear the reaper, our husbands castration,
when we're on our periods together.

For three days or so, we lock ourselves away
We eat sweets, watch *Lifetime* shows, cry and crochet
If anyone lets us out, there's hell to pay
Yes, we're on our periods together.

Now the warning is out, Big Brother has spoken
From San Fran to Tampa, L.A. to Hoboken
Hide kids, pets and anything you don't want broken --
We're on our periods together.

Next week you'll be safe, you can come out from hiding
The mood swings will end, cramps should be subsiding
But start prepping now, 'cause at next month's moon rising…

We'll be on our periods together.

THE HUG

A kind word can cover me
like a warm and cozy sweater,
but a hug from tiny arms
around my middle's even better.

HOUSEKEEPING

Rush rush rush
Faster faster faster
Time is running out

Pick up all the toys
Fold the laundry
and put it away
Wipe down the toilets
and the kitchen sink

Don't forget to dust
the TV stand and all
the photos in the hall

Hurry! Do it now!
There's no time to waste!
It must be done
TONIGHT
because tomorrow

SHE IS COMING

and we absolutely
cannot let
the Cleaning Lady
know
how dirty
we really are

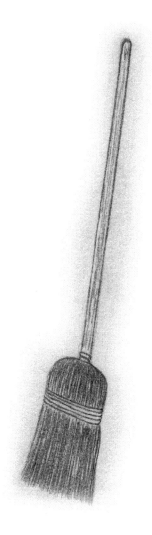

I CAN'T DO MATH

I'm your mom and you should know
I'm always here for you
I'll endlessly support you, son,
in everything you do
If you need help I'll be there, even
long after you're grown,
but when it comes to first grade math...

Kid, you're on your own.

DEATH BY LAUNDRY

It started as a little pile
A little pile of dirtied style
To wash it would just take a while
A very short, short while.

But my life was busy, so
I let it grow, even though
I needed clean and folded clothes
I really let it go.

The family just kept adding more
The hamper spilled out on the floor
Still, I refused to do my chore
That useless, boring chore.

And so the pile became a mound
80 pounds, five feet around
At least six feet, from top to ground
A real impressive mound.

And then it grew into a hill
A silly hill, like Jack and Jill
It grew into a silly hill
A silly, scary hill.

The hill became a mountain then
Tall as Big Ben, and without end
High as a stack of a thousand men
Remarkably tall men.

It grew so tall, it blocked the sun
And without sun, life was no fun
It must have weighed at least a ton
At least a goddamned ton.

Not one clean thing, not anywhere
Our drawers were spare, our closets bare
Not a single pair of underwear!
Not one clean thing to wear.

I fell into the pile one day
Was it foul play? I couldn't say
But I was trapped, to my dismay,
like a needle in some hay.

No help, my husband shook his head
"Tough luck," he said, as I begged and pled
He took the boy and left instead
They left me there for dead.

I began to suffocate
A slow heart rate left me sedate
I thought I could see heaven's gate
I knew death was my fate.

Finally, I felt contrite
"If I'd known, I really might
have separated darks from white,"
I thought, with sad hindsight.

I made one last stab to survive
I kicked and cried, and wished, closed-eyed
That all those clothes were washed and dried...

… and then I fucking died.

MEETING HAIKU: A SERIES

1. Waste of Time Haiku
Instead of meeting
I could be doing the things
we're meeting about

2. Nodding Head Haiku
It looks like I care
about what you are saying
Really not so much

3. Happy Co-Worker Haiku
I am annoyed by
your cheerful ass-kissiness
Take it down a notch

4. Stomach Growling Haiku
I'm not listening
Instead I am wondering
how long until lunch

5. New Ways to Be Productive Haiku
While you were wasting
my time in this lame meeting
I wrote five haikus

DOOMED

Welcome home, little plant
I hope happiness fills you
In the short time you last
before my black thumb kills you.

PERKY MOM

Perky Mom's so friendly
Perky Mom's so cool
Perky Mom's at soccer practice
Perky Mom's at school

Perky Mom is cute
Perky Mom is thin
Perky Mom has not a single
blemish on her skin

Perky Mom gives high fives
Perky Mom cheers the team
Perky Mom is every horny
Perky Dad's wet dream

Perky Mom is perfect
Perky Mom's the tops
I want to squeeze Perky Mom's
perfect head until it pops.

HUSBAND

You drop your clothes onto the floor
right next to the hamper
And off you go, although you know
I'm not a happy camper

You bug me when you know I'm stressed
under the deadline gun
You start projects 'round the house
and leave them halfway done

You're terrible at giving comfort
when I'm sick or sad
You criticize and supervise
and yell when you get mad

You make me crazy
You're way too lazy
You act too proud
You snore too loud
You're rude and abrupt
You interrupt
You're harsh and gruff
You say mean stuff

But...
You're also super cute
with a smile I can't forget,
and you've been crazy sexy
since the first day that we met

You never get embarrassed
and, I have to say,
for all your failings, you still make me
snort-laugh every day

You say things that are tasteless
and your jokes are way too gross,
but your sick mind is what I find
I really love the most

You can find your way around
any problem that you're in,
and you've stuck with me through years
of thick and very thin

Best of all, it's clear that you
adore our little boy
Watching you just be his dad
brings my life such joy

And so, because I love you, and
am grateful for all you give,
I've decided that, at least for now...
I'm going to let you live.

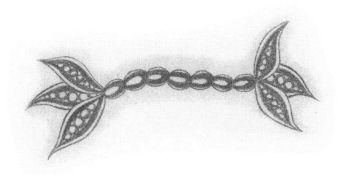

LEAVE THE FUCKING CAT ALONE

You're just a little girl, but still
Leave the cat alone
You seriously need to chill
Leave the cat alone
He doesn't want to play with you
Leave the cat alone
He thinks you're an asshole and I do, too
Leave the cat alone
Why can't you just softly pet him?
Leave the cat alone
He'll scratch you and I swear I'll let him
Leave the cat alone
You'll be hurt, you'll scream and cry
Leave the cat alone
And then I'll laugh, not gonna lie
Leave the cat alone
Just leave the fucking cat alone.

KANYE

I know we all strive to raise our kids
to love themselves just as they are
But I think it's clear that Kanye's mom
went just a *little* too far.

WORLD'S
BEST KID

HAS ANYONE SEEN MY GLASSES?

I know they're here somewhere
I was wearing them before
I think I took them off
right after walking in the door
Without them I can't see a thing
I might as well be blind
My extra fuzzy vision
makes them extra hard to find

I feel around, I stumble
over a sleeping pup
Watch where you're standing,
if you're in my way
you'll likely get felt up

They aren't in my purse
They're not in their case
They aren't on the counter
They're not on my face

They're not even in their usual place
on the table beside my bed…
FUCK! I scream, as I pull out my hair---

Wait.
What's this on my head?

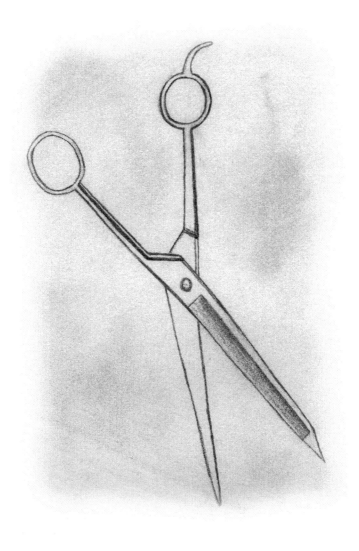

PONYTAIL

Ponytail
Ponytail
You are missing from this head

Just to the
back-and-top hovers
a cold, empty space
where you once sat,
content

Impatience got
the best of me and
I said, in haste,
It's too much - get rid of it
and that's just what the hairdresser did.

I wasn't thinking, I didn't know
how sad I'd be
once you were gone
and now it's too late
and I can't get you back
and I am
left with

nothing

but
Mom
Hair
and
no
motherfucking
Ponytail.

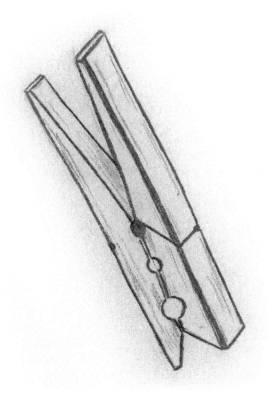

SOMETHING SMELLS LIKE PEE

It wasn't under the kitchen sink
or beneath the EZ chair
I checked behind the fridge again
but it's definitely not there

I pulled the couch out and found
dust mites and an old orange rind
But the thing that I keep searching for
I just can't seem to find.

Believe me, it was rough when I
searched through the laundry pile
(The husband's sweaty workout clothes
had been there for a while)

And when I ventured underneath
my messy toddler's bed
All I found there was dirty underwear
and a severed Barbie head

I asked the father and the son
but both claimed not to know
They looked at me like I was nuts
but I just can't let it go

I've looked and looked but nowhere
can I find what's plaguing me
I won't stop until I find it.

Something smells like pee.

NEIL PATRICK HARRIS
GETS THE PADDLE

In your *Doogie Howser* days
I truly did adore you;
and after *Dr. Horrible*
I'd do anything for you.

How I Met Your Mother still
makes me laugh every time;
and your hosting of the Tonys
was, simply... sublime.

For all this and more, should we ever meet,
I will most sincerely thank you;
But thanks to *Smurfs 2*, the first thing I must do
is bend your ass over and spank you.

RED LIGHT

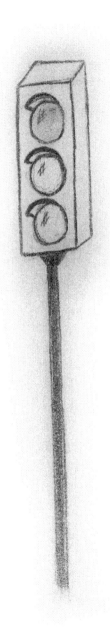

Red light
Stopped too long
Boredom has set in

In search of diversion
I glance to my left
A man looks down
from his huge Hummer perch
He grins as he ogles my legs

A noise from the right
captures my notice
I turn as a man loudly revs
his fancy Corvette engine
He smirks as he revs it again

I look to my left
So tall
So big
I look to my right
So loud
So fast

And I realize that,
at this moment,
right now,

I am the
Meat
in an
Overcompensation
Sandwich.

FUCK THAT DEADLINE

I hear the pool shouting, "Yo! Come swim in me!"
The bikini says, "Hit the gym! A-S-A-P!"
The couch asks, "Hey, wanna come watch some TV?"
And I say to them, "Yes! Fuck that deadline!"

It's the season I spend the most time with my kid
Waterslides have been waiting all year to be slid
He asked me to glide down once more, so I did
And I screamed, "Woo hoo! Fuck that deadline!"

Sandcastles, sno-cones, disc frisbees and beer
Rolling down hills in a big plastic sphere
Gas up the car for a road trip, my dear
The time's here! Right now! Fuck that deadline!

A picnic with pickles and EZ cheeze spread
PB&J on white Wonder Bread
I have my priorities, let it be said.
The ants can all go fuck that deadline.

The park gates have opened, we've trampled inside
All kinds of fun stuff is here to be tried
Roller coasters to ride, bumper cars to collide
And I cry, "It's so fun! Fuck that deadline!"

We're sunburned and tired but continue to go
On the boat, we lay back and just roll with the flow
These days will only come once, dontcha know?
I do, so yeah. Fuck that deadline.

Now I'm home and it's quiet, just the right time
to sit down and write something brilliant and fine,

but *Real Housewives* beckon, the *Bachelor* is primed….
Well, dammit to hell. Fuck that deadline.

Money is tight and we're feeling the pinch, but
I want to enjoy summer's every square inch.
Besides, there's the winter to be a big Grinch.
It's summertime! Yeah! Fuck that deadline!

FIGHT OR FLIGHT

I am sorry
I punched you
in your junk
but you were standing
between me
and the exit
and there was a man
with a chainsaw
coming at me
and a woman
who looked
suspiciously like
Bloody Mary
brandishing a knife
Yes, it was a
Haunted House
and yes, I know
it was pretend, but...
BLOODY MARY, dude.
When I screamed
"I'M FUCKING DONE"
and turned your way to go,
you really should
have stepped aside
but instead you stood still and
now I've escaped and
I see things more clearly and
I'm very very sorry and
I do hope your
penis is
eventually
okay.

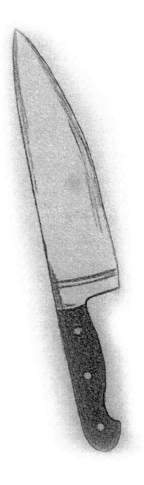

AND NOW, HERE IS AN OCTOPUS WITH A MUSTACHE

Just because.

I DON'T KNOW WHERE
THE MONEY WENT

I don't know where the money went
I think it's all been spent.
I checked our bank balance today and
it's negative nine cents.

I know I used some to pay a few bills
and there's some in the grocery tills
but it seems that's all I did and then
from there it was all downhill.

There *was* that cute little dress that I
saw and just had to buy
And the matching shoes, of course
that immediately caught my eye

And a pair of pearl earrings, super cute
that perfectly matched my bathing suit
I wanted to accessorize poolside, so
I bought a pearl bracelet to boot

Speaking of boots, I found a pair
that perfectly match my hair
I had to buy them, obviously --
Otherwise, what *would* I wear?

Then on the way home, I saw a place
with lingerie made of lace
I bought it, then thought, *You know, I so
need to unwrinkle my face*

So I stopped at the local beauty store
and bought enough Botox for four
but emotion still showed, so I had to go
back there and buy a bunch more

So, I guess I know where the money went
I know where it's all been spent
But at least I'll look cute
when I break the news…
there's not enough left for rent.

PINKLES AND WRIMPLES

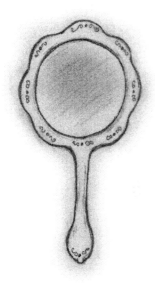

You hit 40 and think,
Now my life will be simple
then you look in the mirror
and find a big pimple.

And you're all,
What the fuck?
Life's not tough enough
with the face sag and age spots
and old people stuff?

A fortune I spend
fighting "Over the Hill,"
now you're saying I also
must buy Clearasil?

This is bullshit, you think.
It's so out of line
to have pimples and wrinkles
at the same time!

40, you suck!
(you think, in disgrace)
If I could, I'd punch you
right in your fat face!

But age brings new wisdom
and you know it's true
that sometimes Life likes to say,
Yeah? Fuck you, too.

LONG-WINDED BOSS

You have said the same thing
twenty different times

I understood the first time
and all the other times
were a waste of my time
and now I have no time
to do the things
you spent that time
telling me to do

over and over and over

OUR HOUSE

It's way too small and our main hall
has a claustrophobic feeling
We hate the tile (it's 80s style)
and the popcorn on the ceilings

We can't afford but badly need
cabinet refacing
There's no storage anywhere
and all the windows need replacing

In the summer it's way too hot
In the winter it's way too cold
Our gutters are all falling apart
Our plumbing pipes are old

It makes us nuts and causes us
huge levels of frustration
But underneath it all there lies
a very strong foundation

Back in 1998
we bought it for a song,
and in '07, we were still here
when our baby came along

It's here we celebrate birthdays
It's here where Santa comes
The backyard's been the backdrop
for tons of family fun

Okay, the garage door's broken,
and sure, our landscape's crappy,
but for the most part, our time here's
been very, very happy

Of course we'd love to upgrade to
a big ranch house or downtown loft...
but it's *sublime* that in two years' time
we'll have this bitch paid off.

It's painful and expensive and
it's long since been outgrown,
but still,
whenever I'm away,
I can't wait to get back home.

THE BLANKIE

Before he was born, the blankie arrived
and through his fourth year, it's survived
Through sniffles and spit-ups and bumps in the night
and long, bouncy, rough late-night drives.

It's been kicked, dropped and thrown,
stopped tantrums before
sweet Jekyll turned into bad Hyde
It's been host to dead bugs and muddy shoe soles
and boogers once picked, but now dried.

Once white, it's now stained a shade of worn-out
with accenting spills and drip-dries
A shell of its former glorious self
after years of the boy's lows and highs.

He's four and a half now, and I know it's time
to bid our sweet Blankie goodbye
But the thought of bedtime without it just brings
a sad, mournful tear to my eye.

The boy is so ready, won't miss it at all –
but it's me who just can't say goodbye.
Because Blankie's been part of our family, you know?
And babyhood's now passed us by.

So *thank you*, dear Blankie, for being his rock
For keeping him warm, safe and dry
I'll now repay you by sending you up
to the cold, damp, dark attic to die.

.

FORKS

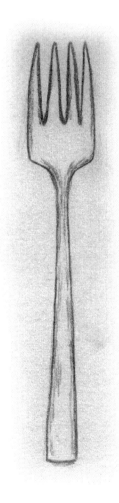

This drawer
was once
full of forks
but now there
are only three.

What ever
happened
to the rest
is a fucking
mystery.

SOCIAL MEDIA

Facebook, Twitter, Instagram
Tumblr, Wordpress, Klout
Foursquare, YouTube, Google Plus
Blogger, Yelp, About
Goodreads, Foursquare, Pinterest
Spotify, Etsy…

What's the point of living life
if everyone else can't see?

LOVE, BUBBLES

SPLENDA IN MY BLENDA

Few things in life are as perfect as Splenda
The stuff's made of magic, I fully intenda
to mix it with rum and some fruit in my blenda
and that night I'll be the world's finest bartenda
(and also everybody's best frienda).

The enda.

SHUT THE FUCK UP ABOUT TWILIGHT

He's sexy and sparkly, all girls' true desire.
So what if he's an old, dead vampire?
It didn't stop Bella from lighting his fire...
but still.
Shut the fuck up about Twilight.

I get it — this story's the stuff made of dreams.
Panties cream, from old moms to young teens.
But these books have been out forever, it seems,
so time's up.
Shut the fuck up about Twilight.

The truth is, you just wish that _you_ could be Bella -
young and dumb, with a rich, gorgeous fella
and an endless love bond, like you're under a spell, but
you're not.
Shut the fuck up about Twilight.

Yes, Edward gets you hot, horny and weepy,
but he's pasty and broody and way too grim reap-y
and a soccer mom pining for him is just creepy.
Grow up.
Shut the fuck up about Twilight.

The last movie's out and I hope that's the end
of the vampire-loves-dumbass-chick trend.
Let's start loving books that don't suck balls, my friend.
Let's all
shut the fuck up about Twilight.

BROKEN

The water heater's broken. The cable's on the fritz.
Refrigerator's hot, not cold. The dog has got the shits.
There's a new noise from the dryer and
I know it can't be good.
The lawnmower broke and weeds are spreading
through the neighborhood.
The guest bath toilet's super clogged. The car is out of gas.
I can't find my keys again, no time to stop for cash.
Late again to work today, the boss is pissed as hell
Told him my alarm clock's broke; he didn't take it too well.
A puddle in the kitchen means
that something's sprung a leak,
But we're not sure what and the plumber
can't come until next week.
The family heirloom tablecloth
is stained with spills of gravy, and –
Oh my god.
Hold everything.

Somebody check the baby!

DEAR MILEY

Dear Miley I know you're young
Dear Miley I know you're cute
I know you're rich and successful
and your fame I can't refute

I know you think you have
something of value to say
But please, for the love
of all that is good...

Put your ass away.

WHERE DID ALL THE LOTION GO

"Where did all the lotion go?"
asked the lady of the fly.
"It's morning, and I need it so!
My skin's so very dry!"

"I use my lotion every day
but lately seem to find,
no matter what I do that bottle's
empty all the time!"

"Could it be a lotion gnome,
who's sneaking in at night?
Or maybe it's a leprechaun
with skin that's dry and tight?"

"Maybe it's a team of thieves
who planned the perfect heist!
Or someone with a grudge!" she said,
"Or a poltergeist!"

"*Who took all my lotion*?!!?"
the lady cried out, loud,
"I'm flaking and I'm itching
and I'll get revenge!!" she vowed.

"I'll bet it was my husband,
playing some cruel trick!
What a jerk!!" the lady yelled.
"He is *such* a dick!"

"Fly, I see you on that wall.
Tell me, was it my spouse?
I need to know, because if so,
I'll eject him from this house."

"Now, now, lady," said the fly.
"Calm down and take a seat.
There's no need to send your poor
man out onto the street."

The fly continued, with a sigh,
"I think that you should try
remembering that, when it's cold,
your skin is extra dry."

"In the winter, human skin
gets scaly to the touch.
That requires moisturizer
be used twice as much."

"So maybe you should take a break
from all this grand emotion,
and instead go to the store
and BUY MORE FUCKING LOTION."

CONTEMPLATING GRAMMAR

If you confuse "you're" and "your"
you'll earn my angry glare

And I'll be pissed if you mix up
"they're" and "their" and "there"

People who can't get "it's" and "its" right
fill me up with hate

But fuck if I know
if I'm "lying" or "laying"
as I contemplate.

OF COURSE YES TO CAMPING

A long, hard struggle
to erect a tent
that will not keep us warm

A fire ban to keep us
freezing in the night

No hot shower to make me clean
No stove to prepare a meal
Big, buzzy bugs everywhere and
no no no
place to poop

Yes, of course YES!
Why WOULD'T I want
to spend
a whole week
camping with you?

I can NOT imagine.

I KNOW YOU HEARD ME

I know you heard me
When I said "STOP"
I know you heard me
When I said "NO"

When I said,
"PUT YOUR PANTS ON NOW"
You heard me.
You did. I know.

And yet,
now there you stand --
nude,
squirt gun in hand

Ready, willing and able
to shoot from your perch
on my table

SQUIRT! The room stills
There is no action
We both take a moment
to process what's happened

I was almost to the count of three,
but then I gurgled helplessly
You squealed giddily with glee

and I wondered as you silenced me
with a stream of squirt gun water --

Why couldn't I have a daughter?

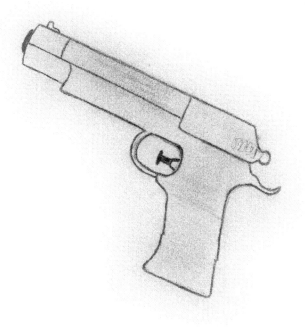

NO-BRAINER

I could stand here
in the kitchen
and scramble eggs badly
and suffer tiny burns
from splattery bacon grease

I could then
wash the pan and my plate
and wipe down the counters
all while tired
and grumpy

Or
I could just eat
that delicious cupcake
with the cream cheese icing
and throw away the wrapper.

Which do you think I will do?

A HAIKU FOR
MY SNOOZE BUTTON

I'm trying to sleep
Nine minutes is an insult
You're so fucking rude.

WHAT THE HELL HAPPENED TO KATHIE LEE?

Was her face run over? Was she stung by angry bees?
Did she ski the slopes too fast and run into some trees?
Perhaps she wound up trapped in a large-scale meat deep freeze?
Or maybe she just suffers severe food allergies.
It could be she's contracted some awful kind of pox –
But I think, maybe, she should just lay off all the Botox.

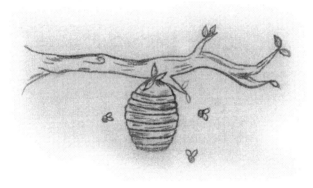

SARCASM

You spilled juice on the floor?
Pretty please let me mop it.

The bathroom faucet's leaking?
I know exactly how to stop it!

You used twelve extra towels?
I can't wait to wash and fold them!

You brought 20 toys with you?
I really want to hold them!

Peed in your bed? In your pants? On the floor?
I'm just sad it isn't poo!

Now, tell me, please --
For you, my love.
What else can I do?

UGLY BABY

Your baby is so ugly
Your baby is so gross
I don't want to touch it
I don't want it close

Please don't make me hold it
or pretend to think it's cute
It scares me, with its face that's so
misshapen and hirsute

I know you love it dearly, and
I think that's very sweet
But, man, that baby's ugly
from gross head to nasty feet

When I look at it I must
suppress the urge to hurl
I can't even tell if it's an
ugly boy or girl

When you hold and comfort it with,
coochie coochie coo,
I stand back and watch and just think,
ew ew ew ew ew

It's not that I don't sympathize
with your situation
I'm truly sorry you gave birth
to such a strange mutation

Still, I can't help thinking…
(not that I'm tracking scores…)
but my own sweet, pretty baby
is *so much* better than yours.

ODE TO THE TOWEL

You clean up my messes,
you soak up my spills,
fresh from the dryer
you chase away chills

In the kitchen, you dry,
clean and cover up treats
In the car, you protect butts
from hot leather seats

At the gym, you wipe sweat
and might act as a mat
In the locker room, you
hide me when I'm feeling fat

I'm a white middle-classer,
a pure-bred Suburban,
but when I wash my hair,
you are my turban

You envelop my son
when he's fresh from the bath
and on wet, slippery tiles
you provide a dry path

Once out of the tub,
while he plays, you're a cape
or a tent (with a couple of chairs
and some tape)

If the boy's diaper-free
he might pee on the floor,
and YOU are the first thing
we always reach for

Wherever I am,
home, office or car,
you're the one thing I need
most often, by far

So thank you, dear Towel,
for supporting our team
and for keeping my hands,
house and son dry and clean

I really love you
There, now I've said it
It's weird, yes, but dude.
You don't get enough credit.

WINTER

I love the cooler temperatures
Hot cocoa, scarves and sleds

But the part that I love
more than anything else...

is not having to shave my legs.

PIE

I wish people would pay more attention to me,
I think,
feeling lonely and sad

Then I shovel
a bite of pie
into my mouth
that is almost
the size of my head

And as I try
to fit my jaw around it
to chew without choking,

I realize
it's probably for the best
that they don't.

CUSS JAR

It seemed like a sensible way
to keep ourselves in check,
to start replacing "shit" and "hell"
with "darn" or "shoot" or "heck"

But in reality it's not
as easy as you'd muse,
and now the cuss jar's overflowed
with tons of IOUs

We'd need a second mortgage
and to sell at least one car
just to pay off what we owe
the motherfucking cuss jar.

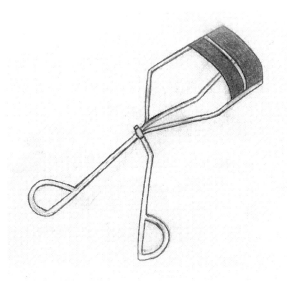

TORTURE

Did I murder puppies?
Did I rob a bank?
Did I stab another person
with a rusty shank?
Did I violate some country's
autocratic rule?

What heinous crime *did* I commit
to get the eyelash curling tool?

I LOVE MY SON

She reminds herself:
I love my son
as he screams "I HATE YOU!"
at the top of his lungs

Again, she says:
I love my son
as he glares at his grandma
and sticks out his tongue

Once more, her mantra:
I love my son
as he breaks things and says
"I was just having fun"

She repeats to herself,
I love my son
as his voice rings out in a
deafening drum
and he scatters a trail of
juice and cake crumbs
and she cleans from her couch
wads of chewed, spit-out gum

But then he hugs her until
her whole neck goes numb,
and she knows that it's worth
all this and then some
She squeezes her eyes shut
and knows that she's won
I love my son
I love my son.

ANNE HATHAWAY MAKES ME UNCOMFORTABLE

So sincere! So earnest!
So very intense!
So wide! So bright! So big! So brown!
So filled with emotion!

It just feels
inevitable
that someday she will turn
those sincere earnest wide bright big brown eyes
in my direction
and all of their intensity
will burn
a gaping hole
deep
into
my
face.

LITTLE DICKS

I know you're little boys
I know you're only six
but if you make my kid cry
I will punch you in your dicks.

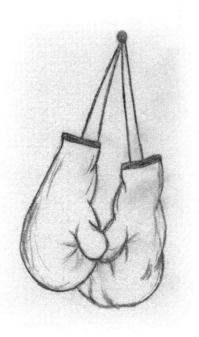

LEARN TO MERGE

You want to merge?
Why yes, of course.
Here, let me just ease back.

Why don't you merge?
Can you not see
I've left room on the track?

Okay, I guess
you've changed your mind
and want to come in
from behind
So I speed up
But you do, too...
and CUT in the goddamned line.

I'm forced to slam
upon my brakes
so hard my coffee flies
Now my car's a total mess
and I'm fit to be tied.

I honk, but you
do not respond
My temper starts to burn

I honk again
Because if not,
however will you learn?

Still there's
no response from you
I shake my fist
in beats of two
Awful words
from my lips spew
I just don't know
what else to do

What happens next,
I can't believe
is what I really see...
As if our roles
have been reversed,

YOU flip the bird
at ME!!

I feel my pulse begin to race
I fight the urge to quicken pace
engaging in a high-speed chase
so I can punch you in the face

But I know that would be wrong,
so I fight the urge

But really,
CUNT
It's time
for you
to learn
to fucking
merge.

I BOTH LOVE AND HATE COSTCO

I just came in for
juice boxes
and some paper towels
and yet, still,
somehow,
I am leaving with

- a Roku
- a flannel robe
- three bottles of wine
- some audio books
- a low-flow toilet and
- an enormous brick of
  cheese

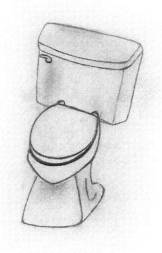

As I check out
you ask me
if I found
everything okay

I look pointedly
at the toilet in my cart
and my $500 receipt

and do not respond.

POISON ARROWS

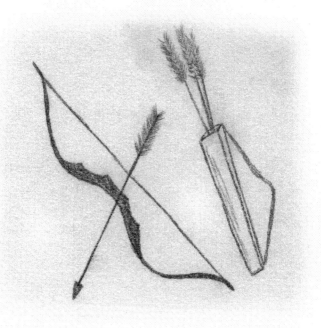

Valentine's Day
Hearts-Candy-Love
Cupid flies about
shooting arrows into
people's asses

Everyone thinks it's *romantic*
but I just see a
War Zone

Duck!
There are fucking arrows!
Fuck!
You got hit in the ass!

That little bastard Cupid
fucking SHOT YOU
with an arrow and it
was tipped with Crazy Poison

And now you've gone nuts
and you truly believe
that the winners of the
Cutest Couples Contest
are actually
"Super Cute!"

and DON'T need
someone to
staple their heads
together.

THE CHOCOLATE MONSTER

Honey, I'm so sorry
but after you went to bed
a huge monster broke in
and punched me in my head

He found your Halloween bucket
and before I could get free,
he picked out all the chocolate
and ate it right in front of me!

I know you're sad now, honey,
I feel so bad for you,
but believe me when I say…
(burp)
There was nothing I could do!

MORNING RADIO

iPod is broken
No satellite
Cannot drive in silence

I switch on the radio and suddenly!
Loud man voices assault my senses!

Loud men talk loudly!
Politics! Religion! Sports!
Rich friends! Hot wives!

Loudly, they laugh!
HA HA HA HA HA!
My hot wife is so dumb!
HA HA HA HA HA!
Fantasy football is so fun!
HA HA HA HA HA!

They talk and laugh
and talk and laugh and
do not know
or care
that their
loud man voices are
sharp
fingernails
scraping
down
the
chalkboard
of my
life.

INS AND OUTS

Dirty clothes IN the hamper
Soiled dishes IN the sink
The garbage IN the trash can
This is easy stuff, I think

And yet, I find these things and more
randomly strewn about
Now, get your shit together
or YOU'LL be what's left OUT.

THE PUPPY

When she gets excited
she pees everywhere
If I leave them out
she will eat my underwear

If she gets out, she will run
and NOT come when you call
She'll stare you down and growl at you
until you throw the ball
If she hears a noise outside
she'll bark and wake us all
She once got trapped in our front room
and *ate the fucking wall, y'all.*

She ate the fucking wall.

She chews my shoes to pieces.
She always tracks in muck.
Yes, she's sweet, and super cute...

but this dog kind of sucks.

HAPPY HOUR

The perky boobs of my twenties
nurse a drink at the bar
My teenaged cellulite-free ass
sits and sips a beer
My flat pre-baby belly
glides in for a gin and tonic
My smooth thirties forehead
sticks with Chardonnay
My upper arm definition
muscles in
and orders a round for the house
and they all raise their cups
in a cheerful toast
to the Good Old Days
when we were all still
One Big Happy Family.

LOLLIPOP IN MY HAIR

There's a lollipop in my hair.
There's a lollipop in my hair.
It's strange how much I do not care
About the lollipop in my hair.

My boy was so happy at first, with his treat
but his body was moving too fast for his feet
and all of a sudden – Fall down! Go BOOM!
For a blip, a dropped pin could be heard in that room.

And then the screams started! And tears shed! Oh, my!
The sobs and the sniffles! The big ugly cry!
His arms wrapped around me and would not let go,
and I would not want them to, no, no, no, NO.

But my neck wasn't all that was clutched by the boy.
He also gripped Lolly like a long lost, loved toy.
And I didn't notice the pushes and presses
as he silently nudged it right into my tresses.

Now the boy is just fine. See him playing out there?
He's running and laughing, without one small care.
I watch him from up here in my cozy chair
as I cling to a still-sticky handful of hair.

Now, there was a day when this might have upset me
I'd have been sad or just let it get me all
Frenzied and flustered and crazed and depressed;
but now it just seems so silly to stress

Because now I have this little boy who
might have sticky fingers, but also can do
things like make me feel better when I'm feeling blue
and make my whole life feel just wonderful, too.

I might have to cut it. It might have to go.
It might be uneven. I might need a pro.
But really, it's hair, and deep down I know
that hair is just hair and back it will grow.

Yes, there's a lollipop in my hair.
There's a lollipop in my hair.
It's strange how much I do not care
About the lollipop in my hair.

ABOUT THE AUTHOR

Blythe Jewell is a freelance writer and editor based in her wonderfully wacky hometown of Austin, Texas. She lives with her husband, son and ever-growing menagerie of pets (which currently includes Andy the Mountain Cat, Jenny the Very Sweet Dumbass and evil genius Napoleon von Weiner).

Her work has been featured in numerous publications both in print and online, and she's won many awards in recognition of her tremendous talent – including an Oscar award, a Pulitzer, the Nobel Peace Prize, a Daytime Emmy and several People's Choice Awards.

She also tends to lie a lot, and enjoys referring to herself in the third person.

For more stupid humor, read her insanely unpopular humor blog *The Bean* at www.themusicalfruit.net. To learn more about her freelance work, visit her quasi-professional, kind-of-grown-up site at www.bejewell.me.

Until then... *shine on, y'all.*

Made in the USA
San Bernardino, CA
14 May 2015